PICTURING THE PAST
Ancient Rome

RICHARD DARGIE

ENCHANTED LION BOOKS
New York

First American Edition published in 2004 by
Enchanted Lion Books, 115 West 18 Street,
New York, NY 10011

Copyright © 2004 Arcturus Publishing Ltd.

Library of Congress Cataloging-in- Publication Data
Dargie, Richard.
Ancient Rome / Richard Dargie.
p. cm. — (Picturing the past)
Includes bibliographical references and index.
ISBN 1-59270-023-3
 1. Rome—Civilization—Juvenile literature. 2.
Rome—Antiquities—Juvenile literature. I. Title.
II. Series.
DG78.D14 2004
937—dc22   2004047222

Produced for Enchanted Lion Books by Arcturus
Publishing Ltd, 26/27 Bickels Yard, 151-153
Bermondsey Street, London SE1 3HA.

Series concept: Alex Woolf
Editors: Liz Gogerly, Margot Richardson
Designer: Simon Borrough
Picture researcher: Shelley Noronha,
                    Glass Onion Pictures

Printed and bound in Italy.

Titles in the series: Picturing the Past
Ancient Egypt
Ancient Greece
Mesopotamia: Iraq in Ancient Times
Ancient Rome

Picture Acknowledgements:
akg-images/Erich Lessing 13 (top); The Art
Archive/Archaeological Museum Naples/Dagli Orti
cover left, /J Enrique Molina 5 (top), /Jarrold
Publishing 5 (bottom), /Dagli Orti 7 (top), /Dagli
Orti 9 (top), /Dagli Orti 9 (bottom), /Dagli
Orti/Museo della Civita Romana Rome 11 (top),
/Musée Luxembourgeois Arlon Belgium/Dagli Orti
11 (bottom), /Archaeological Museum
Naples/Dagli Orti 16, /Dagli Orti 17, /Museo di
Villa Giulia Rome/Dagli Orti 18, /Archaeological
Museum Châtillon-sur-Seine/Dagli Orti 20, /Dagli
Orti 21, /Archaeological Museum Naples/Dagli
Orti (A) 22, /Provinciaal Museum G M Kam
Nijimegen Netherlands/Dagli Orti 23, /Museo
Nazionale Terme Rome/Dagli Orti 24, /Dagli Orti
25, /Musée de la Civilisation Gallo-Romaine
Lyons/Dagli Orti 26, /Dagli Orti 27; Bridgeman
Art Library/Musée Crozatier Le Puy-en-
Velay/Giraudon 13 (bottom), /Merilyn Thorold 15;
Edward Parker/WWF 7 (bottom), Robert
Harding/Nigel Francis 19; The Vindolanda Trust 14
(bottom).
Peter Bull Art Studio *cover right, title page*, 3, 4, 6,
11 (top), 16, 18 (bottom), 20 (top), 23 (top), 24
(top), 26 (top); The Salariya Book Company Ltd 8,
12, 14 (right).

Note to parents and teachers
Every effort has been made by the publishers to
ensure that these websites are suitable for
children; that they are of the highest educational
value; and that they contain no inappropriate or
offensive material. However, because of the nature
of the Internet, it is impossible to
guarantee that the contents of these sites will not be
altered. We strongly advise that Internet access is
supervised by a responsible adult.

Cover art: Gladiator's bronze helmet. Courtesy of The
Art Archive/Archaeological Museum Naples/Dagli
Orti

Contents

Ancient Rome

Rome was the greatest city of the ancient world. It was founded by an Iron-Age people called Latins who farmed and traded in what is now central Italy. Around 800BCE, they built a village and a fortress around seven small hills that lay above the winding river Tiber. The village was named after its legendary founder Romulus. Over time, Rome grew into a powerful city and, under its rulers, called Emperors, Roman armies conquered the other peoples who lived around the Mediterranean Sea. By the year CE100, Rome was the capital of a vast empire that stretched across Europe, Asia Minor and North Africa. The Romans loved their city and called it "Roma, goddess of the Earth without equal throughout the world."

ROMAN EMPIRE
The Romans conquered lands extending from England in the west to Mesopotamia in the east. This map shows their Empire at its greatest extent, in the early part of the second century CE.

WEBLINK
http://www.exovedate.com/ancient_timeline_copyright.html

Look at a detailed timeline of Roman history that traces the rise of the city from a small farming village to becoming the most magnificent city in the ancient world.

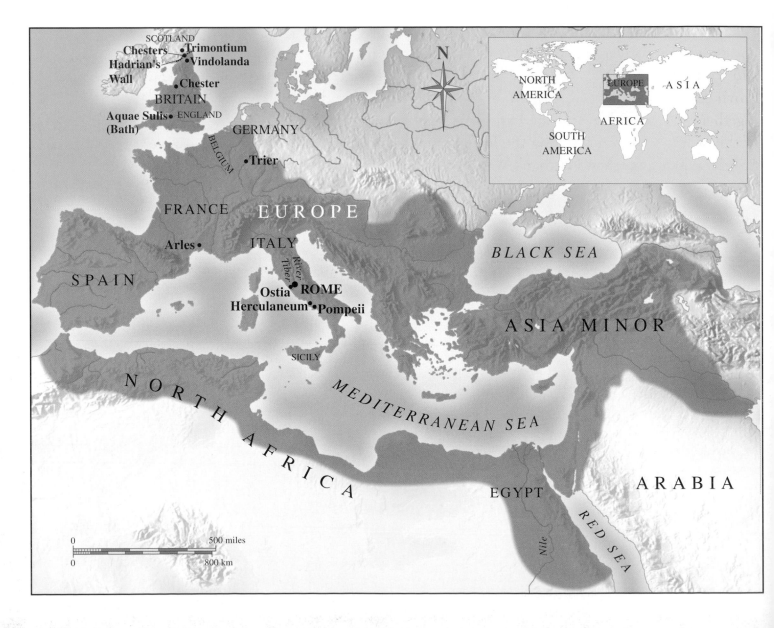

At the height of its power, over a million people lived in Rome. People and goods from every part of the Empire flooded into the city along the straight Roman roads. Inside Rome's walls, the citizens lived in tightly packed, bustling streets, crammed with houses, shops and markets. Grain stores and warehouses lined the docks that ran along the banks of the Tiber. In the center of the city were public buildings made from marble and gold that surrounded the open meeting-spaces of the Roman Forum. Here were the temples, arches, baths and theaters built by Rome's rich and powerful leaders. Towering above them all was the Flavian Amphitheater or Colosseum, where crowds of 50,000 spectators gathered to enjoy the fights between gladiators.

For almost five centuries, the power of Rome brought peace and prosperity to the largest empire of ancient times. Provinces as far apart as Britain and Egypt were bound together by Roman law and the Latin language. The citizens of this world were protected by the legions that manned the frontier defences such as Hadrian's Wall in northern England.

THE COLOSSEUM

The Flavian Amphitheater was built between CE 78 and 80 by the Emperors Vespasian and Titus. One of the largest buildings in the city, it was later given the nickname "Colosseum" because of its huge size.

HOW DO WE KNOW?

All kinds of evidence has survived from Roman times. In Rome and other cities of the empire, such as Ostia and Pompeii, you can still walk along the streets where Romans lived and worked. Many Roman structures have survived, although, like the Colosseum, some of their stone has been used for other buildings. Archaeologists have also found thousands of objects used by Romans in their daily lives. Modern roads often follow Roman routes and Roman place names can be found on any map of Europe. Many books by Roman writers also survive so we can read about the Romans in their own words.

HADRIAN'S WALL

Hadrian's Wall was built between CE 122 and 128 at the order of the Emperor Hadrian. It marked the most northern boundary of the Roman Empire. Beyond it were the Celtic tribes who remained apart from the Roman world.

A Roman Town

A few wealthy Romans lived in palaces and villas but most ordinary people lived in apartment blocks called *insulae* or "islands." Although land in Rome was very expensive, *insulae* were never more than four storeys high. Emperors such as Augustus passed strict laws limiting their height to 69 feet. This was because too many shoddy buildings had collapsed and killed their inhabitants. Unable to build upwards, Roman developers built the *insulae* as close together as possible. This meant that the sun rarely shone on many narrow Roman streets. Dark, shaded streets were perfect places for thieves and pickpockets to operate. Fires could also leap very easily from one building to another.

INSULAE
In some districts of the city, rich Romans from the countryside kept an apartment for when they had business in town. Most *insulae* were in the poorer districts and were heavily overcrowded.

WEBLINK
http://www.ostia antica. org/vinci/vinci.htm

Click on this link to see reconstructed images of Ostia, the coastal port of ancient Rome.

CITY GATES

Most Roman towns had very strong city gates. This is the *Porta Nigra* or "Black Gate" in the Roman city of Trier, now in present-day Germany. It was built to impress the local people with the power of Rome.

STREETS

Stepping stones can be seen in many ancient Roman streets. Some higher blocks were also placed at the side of the streets to help riders mount their horses.

Roman towns were usually built on a grid pattern so that all the streets crossed each other at right angles. The main avenues ran towards the city gates. The streets in a Roman town were well paved and had drains to carry away rain water. There were raised pavements for pedestrians and stone blocks were laid across the roads so shoppers could cross over without stepping in the street dirt. Gaps were left so that wheeled traffic such as carts and chariots could pass.

Traffic jams were common in ancient Rome, especially when builders trundled heavy blocks of stone and marble pillars using wooden rollers. To free up the streets, the first-century BCE ruler, Julius Caesar, ordered all heavy traffic to move through Rome after dark.

HOW DO WE KNOW?

The Roman writer, Juvenal, has left us a vivid description of what it was like to live in a poor district of Rome: "Death comes from every open window as you pass along at night. Look at the height of that roof from which a pot falls and cracks my head… You pray that they will do no more than empty their slop-pails over you… We live in a city shored up on very slender foundations…."

Shopping

Romans liked to walk around the city's markets to see what new things had arrived from the distant provinces of the Empire. They also liked to meet friends and do business in Rome's great trading halls. Markets were not just a place to shop, but a place to see, and be seen, by others.

Trajan's Markets, in Rome, was a large, covered shopping arcade close to the open meeting spaces of the Roman Forum. It was built by the Emperor Trajan in the year CE110. He wanted to build something that would make his name remembered long after his death. His arcade became a famous landmark for Roman citizens and visitors alike. It was built of brick and concrete, but the floors and inside walls were lined with expensive marble. In the hot summer months Romans flocked there to enjoy its cool, shaded halls.

SHOPS
Roman merchants hung out their wares and covered their counters with goods to attract as many passers-by as possible.

WEBLINKS

http://www2.siba.fi/~kkoskim/rooma/pages/TRAJHALL.HTM

http://www.cavazzi.com/roman-empire/tours/rome/trajans-market.html

Investigate the present-day archaeological remains of Trajan's Markets.

On the ground level of the arcade, there were shops selling snacks to passers-by. Above there were rooms and offices that were used by craftsmen and by the government tax collectors.

Many Romans liked to eat while they were out shopping. There were hundreds of *tabernas*, or snack bars, in ancient Rome. These were shops with a space to prepare the food and a cool marble counter to display it on. Popular Roman snacks included slices of roast pork, olives and boiled eggs flavored in spiced water. Most Romans washed these snacks down with honeyed water and fruit juices.

TABERNA
This ancient Roman *taberna*, discovered in Herculaneum, near Pompeii, contains storage jars called *amphorae* as well as a workbench for preparing food.

Some delicacies were kept fresh in *amphorae*, large clay pots full of cold water. *Amphorae* were also used to store all kinds of foods such as wine, olive oil and the spicy fish sauce called *garum* that many Romans loved.

STREET PAVING
This market street in Ostia, near Rome, was paved with mosaics showing pictures to do with trade such as ships and their goods.

HOW DO WE KNOW?

Well-preserved shops have been found by archaeologists at the Roman towns of Ostia and Herculaneum. The shopping arcade at Trajan's Market in Rome also survives. A wall painting at Pompeii shows people enjoying a snack in a *taberna*. Several Emperors issued laws to control the prices of goods in Roman shops. The Roman author Cicero (106-43BCE) wrote about shopkeepers. He despised them because they lied about the quality of their goods. Other writers such as Aelius Aristides (CE117-171) marvelled at the huge range of goods available in the shops of Rome.

D VI IC M SC N RE VI

D VI IC M SC N RE VI

Feeding the Empire

TRANSPORT

Trains of grain wagons drawn by donkeys and oxen were a common sight on the main roads leading into Rome.

WEBLINK

http://www.villa-rustica.
de/intro/indexe.html

Find out more about a typical Roman farm in the first century CE.

By CE100 there were a million mouths to feed in Rome. The city needed huge amounts of food from the Italian countryside as well as from the fertile provinces of North Africa and Egypt.

Much of Rome's food came from farms called *latifundia*. At the center of a *latifundium* was the owner's villa, as well as stables, barns, and cellars for storing wine and olive oil. There were simple buildings where the farm workers lived. Grain and vegetables were grown in the fields around the villa. There were also orchards and vineyards for fruit, and beehives which supplied honey for sweetening food and drinks. Many farms had a *columbarium*, or dove house, which provided a source of fresh meat in the winter months.

The most important crop on a *latifundium* was wheat or corn. This was used to make bread which was given away free to the citizens of Rome. On some farms, donkeys or oxen were used to pull large tools, such as a plough.

HOW DO WE KNOW?

Roman writers, such as Pliny and Virgil, described the life and work of farmers in the countryside. They believed that running a farm estate was the ideal life for a Roman gentleman. Another writer, Lucius Junius Columella, lived in the first century CE. He wrote a set of thirteen books called *De Rustica* which were full of helpful advice for farmers and gardeners. Roman artists often used scenes of country life in their paintings and mosaics. Modern archaeologists have excavated several dozen well-preserved *latifundia* across Europe. Farming tools made of iron have been found in many parts of the Empire.

FARM WORKERS
Much of the hard work on Roman farms was done by slaves. Machines like this *vallus*, or harvester, were only found on the very largest *latifundia*.

WEBLINKS
http://www.gridclub.
com/fact_gadget/
the_romans/the_romans
/farming_and_the_
countryside/

Find out more about the lives of those who lived and worked on the farms that fed the Roman Empire.

Some farms used a crop harvester called the *vallus*. In early Roman times, crops such as wheat were gathered by hand using a sickle. This was slow, hard work. The *vallus* could cut a field of grain much more quickly. Slaves followed behind it, picking up the cut corn and separating the valuable grain from the stalk.

Other farms which were near to Rome mostly grew flowers for sale in the city's markets. Wealthy Romans loved flowers and bought them to strew on their floors when dining with friends. They also placed flowers in their family shrines on holy days.

HARVESTER
Historians used to think the writer Pliny just "imagined" the large harvester drawn by animals. Then, in 1958, archaeologists in Belgium discovered a Roman carving that showed a large crop mower just like the one Pliny described. This model shows how it may have looked.

Moving Around the Empire

WEBLINK
http://web.bham.ac.uk/
leathepd/

Find out more about
the network of Roman
roads in Britain and
how they were built.

The Roman Empire was vast. It was important that there were good roads so that soldiers, messages and goods could move quickly from one place to another.

Roman roads were planned and built by the army. They had to be very well made as they carried a lot of traffic. The road was often laid upon a raised earth embankment. The surface was usually made of three levels. Stone foundations were covered by rough gravel and then by flagstones.

The Romans gave their roads a camber. This means that they were gently sloped to let rainwater run off the surface into ditches at the side. The roads were built very straight to help troops march as quickly as possible along them.

ROAD-BUILDING
Many roads were actually built by soldiers in the Roman army during peace-time, so that the troops were occupied and kept fit. They carried tools such as shovels as part of their equipment.

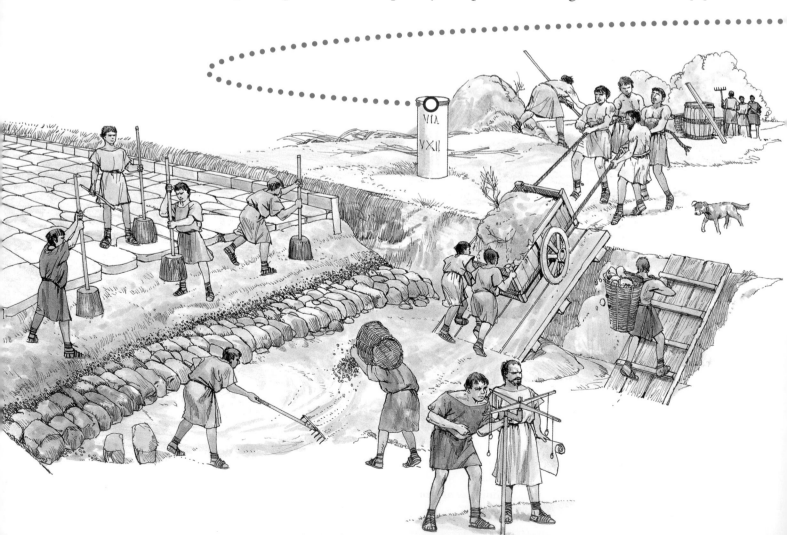

CARRIAGES

Only very wealthy or important Romans could afford to travel in a covered *raeda*. These were comfortable carriages used for long journeys across the Empire.

MILESTONES

Milestones on Roman roads were usually stone pillars, although some were in the shape of square plaques. The inscription told you the distance between the towns where the road started and finished, as well as the name of the Emperor who had ordered the road to be built.

Many modern roads still follow the original routes laid out by Roman engineers. The routes of Roman roads in England, such as Watling Street between London and Chester, can be traced in the present-day landscape. Many inscriptions on Roman milestones give the names of the army officials who supervised the building of the road and say how much the road cost. The Romans also built bridges to carry their roads across river valleys. One bridge in Spain carries an inscription by the Emperor Trajan that proclaims: "I have built this bridge to last for centuries." The bridge is still used by traffic today.

An *agrimensor* or surveyor checked that the road was straight using a *groma* or measuring tool.

Bushes near the road were cut down to prevent ambushes by bandits. At every thousand paces, milestones were put up to tell people how far they had travelled.

Roman roads were fast. A government messenger on horseback could travel as much as 80 miles in one day. Wealthy Romans often travelled long distances in a heavy, covered four-wheeled carriage called a *raeda*. For shorter journeys, Romans used a lighter two-wheeled carriage called the *cisium*.

Along the route there were rest stations where a traveller could buy food and drink and change horses. Many of these stations were like inns, with rooms where a traveller could bathe and rest for the night. There were also special rooms for officials travelling on government business.

By CE100 the whole of the empire was connected by a network of excellent roads. In Britain alone, the Romans built over 9,950 miles of road.

Defending the Empire

When Rome was a small city, everyone was expected to fight when it was attacked. As Rome conquered other lands, a full-time army was needed to defend the empire. In the second century BCE, a Roman general called Marius set up an army of trained men who chose to fight as soldiers for a living. These men usually agreed to serve in the army for long periods of up to twenty-five years. In return, they were paid and equipped by the Roman government.

At its strongest, at around CE50, the Roman army was divided into thirty legions or regiments. Each legion had about 5,000 men. The foot soldier or legionary was heavily armed and well trained. He wore a woollen tunic, and in colder places, such as Britain, a woollen cloak. In battle he was protected by a leather jerkin, covered in iron strips, and an iron or bronze helmet.

SOLDIERS' SHOES
Legionaries wore stout leather sandals that had nails in the soles to stop them wearing out. Many of these sandals, called *caligae*, were so well made they have survived from Roman times.

SOLDIERS
Legionaries carried their equipment in a pack at the end of a pole. The pack contained food rations, a cooking pot and other tools such as a shovel or a pick.

CARVINGS

The carvings on Trajan's Column in Rome celebrate a successful army campaign in eastern Europe. They show legionaries at work building camps and collecting food as well as preparing for battle and defeating a powerful enemy, the Dacians.

HOW DO WE KNOW?

The fourth-century writer, Vegetius, described how soldiers were taught to march in time so they could cover 30 miles a day, and stay together as a disciplined unit. Important Roman army camps, such as Trimontium in present-day Scotland, have also been excavated. Archaeologists have found all the equipment used by legionaries in their daily lives in camp, as well as the armor and weapons they used in battle. Many pairs of well preserved *caligae* were also found at Hadrian's Wall. Although they had been in the ground for over sixteen centuries, the leather had not rotted away.

Roman legions were divided up into units of 80 to 100 men called centuries, led by an officer called a centurion. He was an experienced soldier who had proved himself in army operations and in battle. It was his job to make sure that his men were ready for war. New recruits were toughened up by marching and running in full armor. They practised their weapon skills and strengthened their arms by hurling spears and fighting each other with wooden swords. Shovelling earth to make walls around the camp or helping to build roads also made sure that the legionnaries were fit.

Discipline in the legion was also very strict. Legionaries were flogged or put on half rations or even stoned to death if they disobeyed a command. The first-century writer Flavius Josephus knew that Roman success in battle was due to the discipline and excellent training that centurions gave to their men: "Every soldier in the legion is made to exercise hard every day as if it were war time. This is the reason that the Romans do not tire and stand up so well to their enemies in battle."

WEBLINK

http://fc.nbsc.org/~nbsc7/01/cb footwear.htm

Find out more about the many different kinds of shoes that Romans wore and how the shape and color of your shoes told people how rich you were.

At the Games

GLADIATOR

This gladiator was called *mirmillo* or the "fish man" because of the scales on his armor and helmet. He often fought in single combat with the *retiarius* or "net man," who tried to spike the *mirmillo* with a three-pronged spear called a trident.

The first Romans enjoyed sports such as wrestling and boxing. They competed in a part of Rome called the Field of Mars that was dedicated to the god of war. By the first century CE, however, many Romans enjoyed watching sports such as chariot racing in stadiums like the Circus Maximus. Here vast crowds of about 150,000 spectators gambled and cheered on their favorite chariot teams such as the Blues and the Greens as they hurtled around the .3 mile-long track.

By CE50 there were over 150 public holidays each year in Rome. To entertain the Roman public, Emperors paid for special shows called *ludi* or games. These were held in amphitheaters such as the Colosseum (see page 5) where the gladiators, the men of the sword, fought and often died.

Gladiators were highly trained slaves, owned by rich men who gambled on them to win. Some gladiators were skilled sportsmen who won fame and the wooden sword, the sign of freedom. Others were simply criminals or prisoners of war, who were herded into the arena and fed to wild hungry beasts.

HELMET

Heavy bronze helmets like this protected the head but, once the face guard was locked shut, the gladiator could see very little and was vulnerable to attack from the sides. The helmet of a *mirmillo* often had the shape of a fish on the crest.

AMPHITHEATER
Amphitheaters were built in most large Roman towns such as here at Arles in France. A canvas awning was stretched across as a roof to protect the spectators from the heat of the sun.

WEBLINK
http://depthome.
brooklyn.cuny.edu/
classics/gladiatr/

Investigate the brutal world of the games and find out more about the gladiators and wild animals that perished in the arenas of ancient Rome.

Roman crowds were bloodthirsty and easily bored. They expected to see ever more novel shows in the arena. To win the support of the crowd, emperors spent large sums of money on planning elaborate games. Exotic animals were brought to Rome from different parts of the Empire. A giant bear from what is now the Scottish Highlands was slaughtered on the opening day of the Colosseum. The arena was turned into a maze of trees and bushes in which elephants, rhinoceros and tigers were hunted down. Sometimes, the arena was flooded and gladiators in small ships re-enacted battles from history. Amazons, or women gladiators, were very popular until the Emperor Septimus Severus banned them in CE200. The Emperor Commodus loved the games. He even fought in the arena himself over a thousand times and was proud of his skill at fighting left-handed.

HOW DO WE KNOW?

Several Roman writers such as Seneca (4BCE-CE65) have left a vivid record of the games. One day Seneca went to the arena to watch the gladiators but he was appalled by what he saw there: "It is pure murder. The men have no protective covering and their entire bodies are exposed to the blows... In the morning men are thrown to the lions and the bears, and at noon they are thrown to the spectators who call back the winner of each fight until he is also slaughtered... The result for all of the combatants is death."

17

Relaxing at the Baths

Only a few wealthy Romans had a bath in their own house. Most Romans went to the *thermae* or public baths. Some of the *thermae* were huge. For example, the Baths of Diocletian in Rome could admit about 3,000 bathers at a time. As well as the bathing pools, there were gymnasia, exercise yards, libraries and cool, shaded gardens. There were even stalls where bathers could buy drinks and snacks.

Entry to the baths was almost free. Men, women and children alike were charged just one *quadrans*, which was the smallest Roman coin.

OIL JAR

Instead of soap, Romans cleaned their skin by rubbing oils into it, poured from a small jar. A curved metal tool called the *strigilis* was used to scrape away the oil, sweat and dead skin.

BATHS

Slaves worked all day stoking fires in the basement of the bath house to warm water in large tanks. This was then pumped up into the bathing pools.

Sometimes the Emperor would sponsor the entire cost of a bath-house for a month so that everyone in the city could bathe free of charge. In this way, Romans of all classes were encouraged to keep themselves clean, and diseases were kept at bay.

As well as going to the baths to get clean, Romans also went to meet friends, exercise and relax. The baths were a favorite meeting place. Women went in the morning with the children while men went in the afternoon once their work was done. As well as bathing, Romans could get a massage, exercise at sports such as wrestling, or have their skin scraped by a slave with a *strigilis*.

The Roman writer, Seneca (4BCE-CE65), lived above a small bath-house. He complained bitterly about the noises that came from these baths. He described the groans and hissing of bathers exercising with heavy weights; the loud slapping sounds made as bathers were massaged; the constant chattering of the slaves employed to pluck hairs from the armpits of the bathers, which made the bathers yell; the splashes of bathers jumping into the pools and the cries of sausage dealers and confectioners hawking their wares. Seneca was disgusted by these noises, but his complaints give us a good picture of what a Roman bath-house was like.

BATH

The thermal spring at Aquae Sulis (now the city of Bath) provided about 265,000 gallons of warm water every day. As well as washing and relaxing here, the Romans left small gifts such as coins to Sulis Minerva, the healing goddess of the spring.

At a Villa Banquet

WEBLINK
http://www-2.cs.cmu.
edu/~mjw/recipes/
ethnic/historical/
ant-rom-coll.html

Find out more about
Roman food and try
your hand at preparing
courses for a Roman
banquet.

BANQUET
Romans were allowed
by law to have only a
few guests to dinner.
This was to prevent too
much money from being
spent on banquets, and
to stop people from plot-
ing against the Emperor.

Wealthy Romans liked to invite their friends over for *cena,* or dinner, which was the main meal of the day. *Cena* began in the late afternoon and often lasted for several hours and many courses. The diners relaxed on long couches covered in cushions while slaves poured wine and honeyed water from delicate glass flasks.

JUGS, CUPS AND PLATES
The Romans used pouring jugs and cups made from fine
glass or bronze. They also liked orange-red terracotta
dinner plates, called Samianware, that were made in
Gaul (now France). They were easy to clean and store.

Even in the homes of wealthy Romans, the dining room or *triclinium* was often quite small. There was usually just enough room for three large couches, placed around the walls, which the diners lay on. This allowed the diners to relax, talk quietly and enjoy each other's conversation. The walls of the *triclinium* were painted, or decorated in mosaics made from small pieces of colored stone such as onyx and marble. The pictures on the walls often showed scenes from rich banquets and wild parties, even though most Romans really liked to eat quietly and carefully.

Slaves filled the guests' goblets with wine from a large dish called the *crater*. The food was cut and sliced by a special slave called the *scissor*. Another slave called the *scurra* flattered the guests and announced the toasts. The Romans didn't use cutlery but ate with their hands. So, at the end of each course, slaves brought flasks of oil and water to clean the diners' fingers. After tasting each new dish, the guests were expected to belch loudly as a mark of respect to their host.

HOW DO WE KNOW?

In *Saturnalia Convivia*, Macrobius (c.370-335 CE) described a banquet that Julius Caesar attended in 63 BCE. The menu included: "…sea hedgehogs; oysters; large mussels; field fares with asparagus; fattened fowls; oyster and mussel pasties; black and white sea acorns; sea nettles; roe ribs; boar's ribs; purple shellfish of two sorts. The dinner itself was sow's udder; boar's head; fish-pasties; ducks; boiled teals; hares; roasted fowls; starch pastry."

Learning

STUDENTS

This portrait shows a couple from Pompeii in the first century CE. The woman holds a set of wax tablets and a thin stylus while the man holds a papyrus scroll. These signs of learning were deliberately included to show that the couple were well educated.

WEBLINK

http://www.history learningsite.co.uk/roman _education.htm

Go to this site to find out more about daily life for the few Roman children who did attend school.

Very few Roman children went to school. They were expected to learn from their parents instead. As a result, most Romans were unable to read and write. Girls were seldom taught these skills. They were trained in the domestic tasks of weaving, cooking and running a household. Only the sons of wealthy families were given a proper schooling. They were taught to read, write and count. They also learned useful things for later life such as law, business and how to speak well in public.

HOW DO WE KNOW?

Thousands of pieces of Roman writing have survived from ancient times. Many were meant to survive, such as the inscriptions on buildings like the Pantheon temple in Rome, or on monuments such as Trajan's Column. Other pieces of writing that survived by accident often tell us about the daily life and routine of ordinary Romans. Pieces of a letter found in a pit at Vindolanda Fort, in northern England, tell us that one Roman soldier was grateful for the warm clothing that his mother had sent him. In Pompeii, the rude graffiti scrawled on buildings also reminds us that the Romans had a sense of humor.

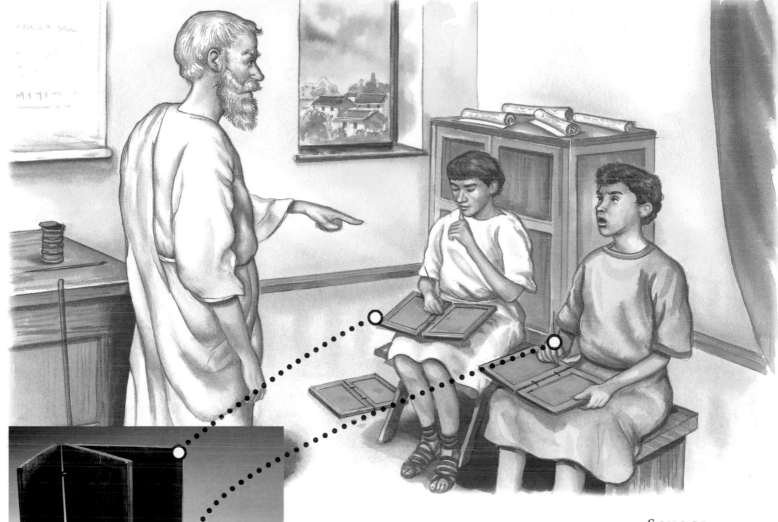

WAX TABLET

Writing tablets were wooden rectangles which were hollowed out in the middle and filled with wax. Sets of tablets were closed up like a book and tied together with string. The bronze stylus and inkwell next to these tablets date from the time of Emperor Nero (CE54-68).

SCHOOL

Tutors were often well educated slaves. They had a reputation for being very strict. One popular Roman saying was: "A boy who has not been caned has not been trained."

Children usually learned to write using wax tablets. They wrote their letters in the soft wax using the sharp end of a bronze stylus or needle. They rubbed out their mistakes by smoothing the wax with the other, broader end of the stylus. Boys who were destined for jobs in government also had to learn to write on papyrus. This was a kind of yellow paper made from a plant that grew in Africa and Asia. Writing on papyrus was done with a reed pen with a split nib, which was dipped into a small bottle of ink made from vegetable dyes, soot and sepia from cuttle-fish.

In later Roman times, boys went to school from the age of seven to fourteen. The school day started very early in the morning, often at dawn. The writer Martial (CE38-104) lived near a school and complained about the noise coming from it every morning: "Oh cursed schoolmaster, what right do you have to disturb everyone before the cock crows with your savage threats and beatings?"

Worshipping the Gods

OFFERINGS
Bulls were often sacrificed to Jupiter, king of the Roman gods, because they were the strongest and most valuable animals that the Romans possessed.

The Romans worshipped many gods and believed they could win their favor by offering gifts to them. Every day a Roman family would lay fruit, cakes or flowers on the *lararium* or shrine to their own family gods and spirits.

The Romans also sacrificed valuable animals to the gods. Stone altars were usually placed outside so that the spirit of the sacrifice could rise to heaven. Mysterious priests called *haruspices* examined the insides of the animals for signs of good fortune. The Emperor Augustus himself sacrificed a bull in 17BCE, saying the following prayer: "O Jupiter, Best and Greatest of the Gods! May every good fortune come to the Roman people thanks to the sacrifice of this splendid bull."

ALTARS
Roman altars were either square or round. They were often decorated with flowers. On religious holidays they were festooned with garlands of flowers.

WEBLINK

http://www.durham.
anglican.org/parishes/
sadberge/altar.html

Find out about the
recent accidental
discovery of a Roman
sacrificial altar.

Different gods and goddesses were worshipped at different times of the year. The Roman year began on 1 March with the lighting of the sacred flame of Vesta, the goddess of the hearth. Games and sacrifices were held in early April for Cybele, the Mother Goddess. April was also the month of festivals for Ceres, the corn goddess. Women played a big part in the ceremonies for Flora, the goddess of flowers, which lasted from 28 April to 3 May each year. The most important festival in the year was for Jupiter, the Father God of the Roman people. It lasted for two weeks in September.

On 17 December, the Romans enjoyed a holiday called Saturnalia. After worshipping the god Saturn in his temple, all Rome feasted on pigs and gave gifts of pickled fish and prunes to their friends. At the end of the year, in February, a dog and a goat were sacrificed in the festival of Lupercalia to the spirit of the She-wolf who had fostered Romulus and Remus, the legendary twin founders of the city.

SHRINE
Most Roman homes had a *lararium* or shrine. It was often shaped like a small temple and placed near the main doorway. This one, from Pompeii, shows a sacred snake which was a sign of good health and fertility.

HOW DO WE KNOW?

Many Roman temples and statues of gods have survived. Archaeologists have also found the special knives and bowls used by priests when making sacrifices. Altars to the Roman gods have even been found outside the Empire, in Germany and Scotland. This suggests that the Roman army carried altars with them on their campaigns. The names of the months also remind us of Roman religion. January comes from Janus, the two-headed god who guarded the entrance to Roman houses. February takes its name from the Lupercalian ceremonies. The noble youths who took part in this festival cut strips of hide called *februa* from the sacrificial goat. March was the month of Mars, the god of war, while June belonged to Juno, Queen of the Gods.

City of the Dead

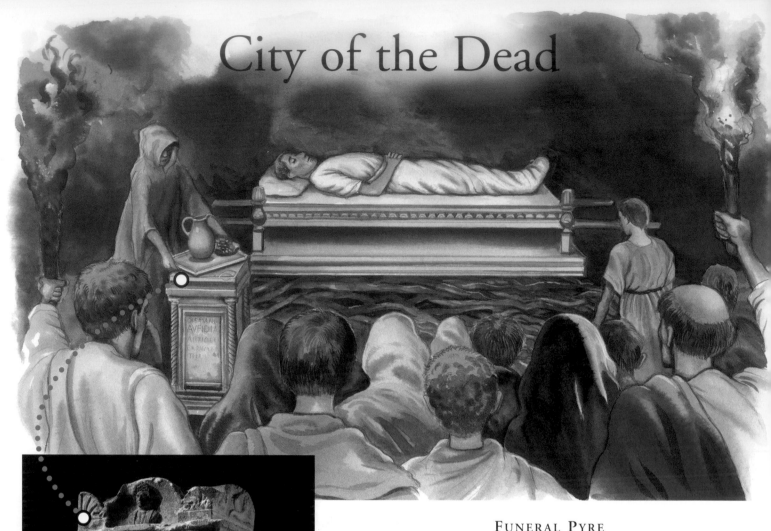

CREMATION STONE

During the funeral of a wealthy Roman, the priest offered gifts to the gods on a small alter.

FUNERAL PYRE

Roman families carried their dead on a litter to a wooden shrine called a pyre. After the sacred ceremonies, the nearest relative lit the pyre with a burning torch to cremate the body.

It was strictly forbidden by Roman law to bury the dead inside the walls of the city. The dead were carried to the fields outside and placed in tombs by the road. For many miles on either side, thousands of tombs lined the main roads into Rome. Underneath were the catacombs, huge underground cemeteries where Roman Christians placed their dead.

Roman funerals usually took place in the middle of the night. The mourners carried burning torches called *funes* and wore masks made from a wax cast of the dead person's face. A coin was placed in the mouth of the corpse. This was to pay Charon, the mythical ferryman. It was believed that he would carry the spirit of the dead across the river Styx to Hades, the world after death, also called the "Kingdom of the Shades."

TOMB
Many wealthy Roman families decorated the insides of their tombs with fine wall paintings. They also left jugs of food and wine to accompany the dead person on the journey to the next life.

WEBLINK
http://www.ku.edu/ history/index/europe/ ancient_rome/E/Roman/ Texts/secondary /SMIGRA*/Funus.html

Investigate Roman burial customs and their superstitions about the dead.

Romans usually burned or cremated their dead. If the family was wealthy, the ashes were placed in a tomb. Poorer Romans often bought a niche, a shelf space, in a building called a *columbarium*, like a dove house. These were large domed buildings with hundreds of small niches for cremation pots. After CE50 increasing numbers of Romans were converting to Christianity. They believed they would need their bodies after death when they went to heaven. So they buried their dead in the cata-combs. These were deep tunnels cut into the soft rock of the Roman countryside. The Christian dead were wrapped in linen covers, called shrouds, and laid out on shelves to await their resurrection or rebirth.

HOW DO WE KNOW?

Many Roman tombs have survived and we can read the writing on them. Many of these inscriptions are still sad to read today: "To the eternal memory of Blandinia, our blameless girl who lived only ten years, six months and sixteen days, this tomb is raised by her parents who miss her laughter." Other tomb inscriptions contained a warning: "Passerby, you see me as a corpse but I was Apollonis who won the athletic games eight times but met my fate in the ninth boxing match. Laugh, but remember that you too must die and join me in Hades."

Timeline

A NOTE ABOUT DATES

All the dates in this timeline are BCE dates. This stands for "before the Common Era." BCE dates are counted back from the year 1, which is taken to be the beginning of the Common Era (CE). There was no year 0. These dates work in the same way as BC (before Christ) and AD (*Anno Domini*, which means "the year of our Lord"). Some dates have the letter "c." in front of them. This stands for *circa*, which means "around." These dates are carefully calculated guesses, because no one knows all the exact dates of events in ancient times.

c. 800BCE Archaeologists believe that the Latins founded Rome.

753BCE Romans believe Romulus founded the city.

510BCE Romans expel their kings and Rome becomes a republic (with people voting for their government rather than having a king).

312BCE Romans begin building the Appian Way, the most famous Roman road.

c. 200BCE Rome is the strongest power in the Mediterranean world.

c. 120BCE First use of concrete in Roman buildings.

112BCE First fire brigade set up in Rome to help combat fires in its crowded streets.

146BCE Roman legions destroy the rival city of Carthage in North Africa.

109BCE Marius sets up a new Roman army of professional legionaries.

63 BCE Marcus Tullius Tiro invents Roman system of shorthand writing.

46BCE Romans adopt the Julian Calendar of 365 and a quarter days.

45BCE Julius Caesar becomes dictator (a ruler with total power over the Roman world).

44BCE Caesar murdered by supporters of the old Roman Republic.

31BCE Romans conquer Egyptian Empire, which becomes a Roman province.

27BCE Octavian (Augustus) becomes ruler of the Roman Empire.

25BCE Agrippa builds 985 foot-long aqueduct at Nîmes in France.

20BCE The Golden Milestone showing the distance between Rome and other cities of the Empire set up in the Roman Forum.

CE14 Death of Augustus.

CE43 Roman invasion of Britain.

CE50 Christianity spreads from Palestine to Rome.

CE79 Destruction of Pompeii and Herculaneum by the volcano of Mount Vesuvius.

CE80 Opening of the Flavian Amphitheater or Colosseum.

CE110 Trajan begins the construction of his vast forum and market.

CE117 Roman Empire reaches its largest geographical extent.

CE122 Hadrian orders construction of a wall across northern England, which is now known as "Hadrian's Wall."

CE166 Roman ambassadors reach the court of the Chinese Emperors.

CE192 Death of Commodus, the "gladiator" Emperor.

CE200 Septimus Severus bans women from fighting as gladiators.

CE216 Baths of Caracalla opened.

CE325 Constantine bans public gladiatorial combats.

CE330 New capital of Roman Empire built at Constantinople.

CE335 Christianity becomes official religion of Roman Empire. First Christian Cathedral of St. Peter's built at Rome.

CE337 Constantine the Great baptized on his death-bed, becoming the first Christian Emperor.

CE364 Romans pass law against magicians, who were seen as dangerous and untrustworthy.

CE367 Northern tribes of Picts and Scots smash Hadrian's Wall and invade southern Britain.

CE380 Romans invent a water-powered saw for cutting marble stone.

CE400 Roman legions in Britain withdrawn and sent to help other parts of the Empire under attack.

CE408 A nomadic people called the Visigoths invade Italy.

CE410 Rome sacked by Goths under the leadership of Alaric.

CE452 Roman legions win their last great victory defeating Attila the Hun at Châlons in Gaul.

CE476 End of Roman Empire in Western Europe.

CE527 Justinian, the Roman Emperor in the East, abolishes the old pagan gods of Greece and Rome.

CE1453 End of Eastern Roman Empire in Constantinople.

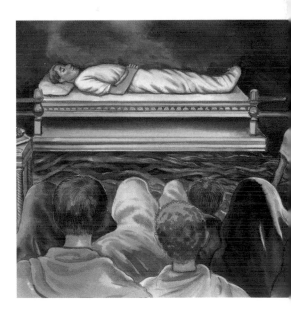

Glossary

Amphitheater A large stadium, where Romans went to watch gladiators fighting.

Aqueduct A long channel bringing fresh water from the hills into the city, often raised up on high arches and towers.

Arcade A covered passageway of arches where Romans walked when shopping or sheltering from the weather.

Archaeologist A person who finds out about the past by looking for the remains of buildings and other objects, often beneath the ground.

Armor Metal coverings used by soldiers to protect parts of the body during battle.

BCE Used in dates. Means "before the Common Era."

Bronze A hard metal made by mixing copper with tin.

CE Used in dates. Means "the Common Era." The Common Era begins with year 1, which is the same as the year AD1 in the Christian calendar.

Chariot A light carriage, usually two-wheeled, used by the Romans in battle, in racing and to carry important people in processions.

Christian A follower of the first-century religious leader Jesus of Nazareth, called the Christ or "anointed one."

Emperor The name given to the ruler of the Roman world in the period between the first emperor, Augustus, in 27BCE and the last, Romulus Augustulus, in CE476.

Empire The many lands conquered by the Romans and ruled by them as one state.

Flogged Beaten with a whip or a stick.

Forum A large open space in the center of a Roman town where important meetings and ceremonies took place.

Gladiator A professional fighter, usually a swordsman, who fought in the public arena.

Graffiti Drawings or words scratched or painted on to the walls in Roman towns, often funny or rude.

Jerkin A short, close-fitting jacket, often made of leather, and worn by Roman legionaries under their armor.

Mosaic A picture or pattern made with many small pieces of colored glass, stone or tile.

Pyre A pile of burnable material, such as wood, used to cremate the remains of the dead.

Romulus and Remus Legendary brothers who, as babies, were raised by a she-wolf and later founded the city of Rome in 753BCE.

Sepia A brown colored pigment made from an inky liquid produced by cuttlefish.

Slave A person who is owned completely by another, often a prisoner of war or bought in a slave market.

Stadium A large open-air building where Roman sports such as chariot-racing took place, with banks of seats for spectators.

Temple A holy building which the Romans believed was the home of a god, where priests carried out religious ceremonies.

Tomb A monument containing the body of a dead Roman.

Tunic A loose, short, one-piece garment that covered the upper body and upper legs, often drawn in or belted at the waist.

Villa A Roman country house, usually built at the center of a farming estate.

Further Information

Books to read
Ancient Rome (Eyewitness Guide) by Simon James (Dorling Kindersley, 1990)

Gods and Goddesses: In the Daily Life of the Ancient Romans by Peter Hicks (Hodder Children's Books, 2003)

History Starts Here: The Ancient Romans, Anita Ganeri and Michael Posen (Hodder Wayland, 2003)

History Makers: The Romans by Clare Oliver, (Parragon Publishing, 2002)

I Wonder Why Romans Wore Togas and Other Questions About Ancient Rome by Fiona MacDonald (Kingfisher Books, 1997)

Illustrated World History: The Romans by A. Marks and G. Tingay (Usborne, 1992)

Look Inside a Roman Villa by Richard Dargie, and Adam Hook (Hodder Wayland, 2002)

Roman World: Pompeii by Peter Connolly (Oxford University Press, 1990)

The Romans (British Museum Activity Book) by John Reeve and Patricia Vanags (British Museum Press, 1999)

See Inside A Roman Town by J Rutland and RJ Unstead (Kingfisher Books, 1986)

Time Tours: A Visitor's Guide to Ancient Rome by Lesley Sims, Christyan Fox and Ian Jackson (Usborne, 1999)

Time Traveller: Rome and Romans by Anne Civardi, Heather Amery, and Simon Courtwright (Usborne, 1997)

Usborne Internet-linked Encyclopaedia of the Roman World by Jane Bingham, Fiona Chandler, and Sam Taplin (Usborne, 2001)

CD-ROMs
Build a Roman Town (Anglia Multimedia Ltd, 1998)
Real Romans (English Heritage Education Service/TAG Learning Ltd, 1999)
Romana (J-PROGS, 1998)
Romans (Anglia Multimedia Ltd, 1994)
Romans (Two-Can Publishing, 1998)
Romans (Graphyle Publications, 1998)

DVDs
Ancient Civilizations: Rome and Pompeii (Questar Inc, 2001)
Lost Treasures of the Ancient World – Ancient Rome (Cromwell Productions, 2003)
The Roman Empire in the First Century (David Grubin, 2002)

VIDEOS
Ancient Rome – A Journey Back In Time (Cromwell Productions, 1998)
I Caesar – The Men Who Ruled The Roman Empire (Beckmann Visual Publishing, 1999)
Pompeii – A Journey Back In Time (Cromwell Productions, 2000)

Index